Lawn Art, Kansas

by Lu Duerksen and Kathryn Nelson

PBS

PARTNERSHIP BOOK SERVICES

Lawn Art, Kansas
© by Lu Duerksen and Kathyrn Nelson

First Printing, 1996
Printed in the United States of America
Produced by: Partnership Book Services, 212 N. Ash, Hillsboro, Kansas 67063

Cover Photograph – Lu Duerksen, Co-Author
Cover and Content Design – Denise Brueggeman-Siemens, Mennonite Press

ISBN 0-9645085-8-3

Duerksen, Lu.
Lawn Art, Kansas / Lu Duerksen, Kathy Nelson.
p. cm.
Preassigned LCCN: 96-69167
ISBN 0-9645085-8-3

1. Fold art--Kansas--Pictorial works. 2. Lawns--Kansas--Pictorial works. 3. Landscape architecture--Kansas--Pictorial works. I. Nelson, Kathryn M. II. title.

NK810.K3D84 1996 709.781
QBI96-40140

Lawn Art

BY LU DUERKSEN AND KATHRYN NELSON

The house itself was not uncommon for the neighborhood, a simple bungalow painted sky blue with perky white trim. It was the profusion of lawn ornaments and other decorations that distinguished the house from its neighbors on the block. Like a color snapshot that refuses to fade, the image of this house remains vivid in my early childhood memories.

I recall the yard a wonderland, brimming with statues, windmills, shiny glass and colorful plastic things. Large and little, square and round things. Singular items and groupings. Twirling things hanging from the porch and sprouting from the ground. The red, white, yellow and other bright colors enticed me as we drove past that house on those long-ago trips to grandma's.

To a child, the yard and house evoked feelings of cheer, even in the dreary gray of a Kansas winter. My secret wish was to stop the car so I could play in that happy yard, although I never told my parents. I understood, somehow, that this yard was not for children to play in, but only to look at. I also suspected that adults might not see it in quite the same light that I did. To them the yard decor was probably divergent and eccentric rather than gay and exciting.

Many things change as we grow up. That house from my childhood is now painted white. Different pieces in the yard have been added or lost. But the impact of that marvelous yard remains the same. People still notice the house and its ornaments. I'm sure children still wish to play there.

To this day, while driving past other homes, I am fascinated by the things displayed in front yards. My sense of appreciation for lawn decoration is pleasantly linked to those early memories. Over time, I've become a devotee of this unique form of artistic expression known as lawn art.

Recently, my friend and co-author Lu Duerksen and I came across a yard displaying a stunning assortment of lawn art pieces. We were so impressed by the variety that we turned around and parked the car in order to fully appreciate the entire artistic scene. I think it was the sun, glinting off the rows of blue glass insulators that recalled my life-long interest in this unrivaled art form. For years I had toyed with the notion of a book, a formal recognition of lawn art. I mentioned the idea to Lu who instantly replied, "OK, I'll start taking pictures for it tomorrow. Which house is first?"

You can guess my answer.

We began our documentation by locating specific items we remembered from weekend trips and drives through town. Our friends willingly jotted down addresses of interesting lawn art they had seen going to and from work or the grocery store. Locating lawn art was not difficult. The more you look, the more you see. In fact, I became a bit of a driving hazard as my attention became overly focused not on the road ahead but on potential lawn art two blocks ahead.

We discovered that if we found one home displaying lawn art, several other homes in the same neighborhood would also have art in their yards. We also observed styles of lawn art to be somewhat consistent within a neighborhood. In some areas birdbaths are the predominant art form. In other areas one finds a selection of religious grottos. Often lawn art is contagious within a neighborhood. If a windmill sits in one yard, two more can be easily found nearby. It would appear that lawn art displays may have some relationship to "keeping up with the Jones." Almost every socio-economic group displays a form of lawn art. Unfortunately, strict covenants limit creative lawn art expression in some neighborhoods.

As we became acquainted with different forms of lawn art, we identified unusual pieces of art as well as certain trends. There are the standard pieces with which most people are familiar such as the donkey and cart, flamingos and Madonnas. Even these pieces are far from mundane in that owners express their personal tastes by painting them, planting flowers in the cart or surrounding it with rocks. There are one-of-a-kind pieces such as a totem pole, a bowling ball on a pedestal, or a washtub on a stand set over an old coffee pot with an American flag stuck in the spout. Each time we found these unusual pieces, we felt like we had won the lottery. The excitement of the finds became addictive and we wanted more.

Not only did we photograph the pieces, we also talked to the artists. We wanted to know the "why" and "how" of their lawn art acquisitions. As Lu suspected, lawn art owners were usually eager to talk to us and have their works photographed. Most people were delighted that their creations were considered significant by others. At worst, some people thought our project strange, but obliged us anyway.

In the process of compiling this book, many personal stories about lawn art unfolded. A favorite tree trunk-shaped cookie jar became too chipped to use, but the owner could not bear to throw it away. Instead, the jar was promoted to a position of art by displaying it in the flower bed. In the shady corner of a yard, a unique grouping of whimsical figurines grew out of defeat: no matter what he planted, the owner could not get any plants to grow there. In the end, lawn art triumphed over nature.

In recognizing the skill, craft or creativity in human effort, the otherwise mundane can be seen as art. By nature and by profession, a teacher, I am inclined to see people and their undertakings in the best possible light, to find beauty in intention, if not in the product itself. To fully appreciate lawn art, such a philosophy is helpful.

It is with this same sense of enjoyment that we offer this book, and hope that you will capture the spirit of lawn art as it dwells in our memory and thrives in the community.

— *Kathryn Nelson*

ACKNOWLEDGEMENTS

Lawn Art, Kansas represents the fulfillment of an idea Kathy tossed out about three years ago. To actually have accomplished the feat of getting a book published seems like a dream. As I invested more and more time in the project, I knew the information needed to be seen by the public. I also realized that completing this project would mean much to me; something like having children means to others.

My thanks go to Kathy for having this idea and of course to Hilary for putting up with us when we worked on the project. I appreciate the support of my friends who have watched this project grow and have encouraged me -- Kathyrn and Dan Coronado, Mark, Joan, and Dave Wasser; Myron, Phyllis, Andrea, and Emily Regier Voth; and Dave and Melinda Hill.

Thank you also to DeeAnn Dubiel, Danny McKinney, Debbie Williams, Mike Dorsey, Richard and Terry Bartel, Mike Floodman, Jennie Wyant, Nancy Erckenbrack, Kathy Mischke, and Andrea Miles for their kind, gentle, continued interest and support with this project.

A very special thank you to Lois and Clark. They shall be rewarded with an extra doggie biscuit for their tolerance and continued home guide duty while their mother was away taking pictures.

— *Lu Duerksen*

There are many to thank, family and friends, for their support and encouragement along the way (especially Mac and Pup. Thanks for the hippo, Mac). And Lu kept pushing, thank goodness, or this project wouldn't have happened. But mostly I owe a great deal of gratitude to my daughter Hilary who spent countless hours in the backseats of our cars as we traveled to unknown places in search of lawn art. I am thankful that she has a heart big and kind enough, even for a little girl, to patiently appreciate the whims and fancies of others, especially her mother. And Abby, too, caught the spirit and brought "Pinky the Christmas Cat" into my life. Thanks.

— *Kathyrn Nelson*

TABLE OF CONTENTS

Burrton Gnomes

INTRODUCTION

$\mathcal{L}$awn art is an overlooked form of creative expression. Professions are devoted to the arts of interior design, landscape design and architecture. An interior designer may include lawn art as part of patio design and a landscape designer will likely add lawn art to the yard. An architect's plans will often include outside ornamentation but in all these cases, lawn art is one part of a whole.

Lawn art deserves a category of its own. It is a genre of art for the common man and the manipulation of color, forms, texture and design serves to delight the creator as-well-as those passing by. The artistic expressions of traditional fine art forms, folk art or home decorating, are personal expressions that can be viewed under conditions set forth by the artist. Lawn art, on the other hand, is a personal expression exposed for all to view and appraise. Although this form of art risks ridicule, the artist finds pleasure in its creation and deserves notice.

Lawn art is usually easy to understand and appreciate and to many, it provides a point of reference to something visually pleasing. The responses vary: "Have you seen the flamingos that guard the Madonna on 34th Street?" or, "When I was young, there was a house on the corner with a huge plaster dog holding a basket of flowers." The recollections are pleasant and these stories are eagerly shared.

Specifically lawn art may be defined as any singular item, collection or arrangement of items, made or acquired by the artist, that is located outside the house and used for aesthetic purposes. Some lawn art may also be categorized as folk art, naive art and, if sculpted by a professional artist, fine art. Yard art can range from a simple singular item, such as a small wood cutout bunny, to a yard packed with an array of items. We discovered that many arrangements are made without adherence to "rules" regarding theme, color, texture or proportion. Groupings frequently are a result of spontaneous additions to on-going collections. This by no means is a criticism. This is what makes lawn art so delightful.

So often traditional art criticizes society. People, in turn, are critical of art. Others find art intimidating. It may be held aloft from and seem unobtainable to the layman. While people who have lawn art generally do not consider themselves artists, in a sense they are. The yard is their palette. Their message is enjoyment. Lawn artists seldom critique or criticize another's work. At most they may express some envy over a prized piece in a neighbor's yard. The general attitude amongst lawn artists is simply "anything goes." It is the joy of creation and the pleasure of display that is the artists motivation as well as the end result.

Of course, for some, money is a motivational factor for the creation and display of lawn art. This holds true especially for faddish wood cutouts, like the giant painted butterflies that adorn many houses and gardens. Retirees make up a significant portion of lawn art exhibitors and vendors. Creating and selling lawn art offers not only something to do, but a few extra dollars as well. Aside from cottage industrialists, most lawn artists are exceedingly generous. If a piece of art is admired, owners often refer the admirer to places where a like item may be purchased. Some people freely offer to make a copy of their favorite item for those who request it.

Lawn art pieces generally have a personal history. How it was acquired, the purpose of its placement in the yard, and the sentiment it brings to the owner are all part of the message of lawn art. This art form also has a general history that spans centuries.

This sundial is found in a church yard. The pedestal is as much a work of art as is the sundial.

History
C H A P T E R   1

Lawn art has been around for about as long as people have maintained permanent living quarters, and in particular, gardens. During times of stability and relative prosperity, gardens became more than a matter of production and consequent survival. The garden became a place of pleasure, with the inclusion of architectural and artistic ornamentation. At various times throughout history, artistic masterpieces have been created for gardens (Plumptre, 1989).

There is evidence, although scarce, of ornamental gardens created by the early Mesopotamian civilizations. These in turn influenced the early Egyptian gardens which incorporated statues of sphinxes, kings and deities. The enduring popularity of urns and vases and statues of goddesses and heroes stems back to the time of the early Greeks. Japan, China and ancient Persia also left their mark on gardens and garden ornamentation (Plumptre, 1989).

It was the Italian Renaissance, however, that established the ornamental garden in the west, incorporating statues, urns and fountains in the landscape. The first such garden, the Cortile del Belvedere in the Vatican, was designed in Rome in 1503 by Bramante, commissioned by Pope Julius II. The centerpiece of the garden was a display of the Pope's collection of antique statues. The French expanded on the Italian concepts, as did Germany, England and the rest of Europe (Plumptre, 1989).

THE SUNDIAL WAS GIVEN AS A GIFT IN THE MEMORY OF A LOVED ONE.

Arriving with the earliest settlers in American, came the influence of European gardens. But neither statues nor fountains were a part of early American gardens. It was not until after the Civil War, when America's wealth and power grew, that formal gardens including ornamentation became a part of the "Country House Era" (Plumptre, 1989). Aside from the commissioned formal gardens of the wealthy, however, there has always existed a more intimate form of garden decoration, better known as folk art.

An early American influence that remains a common lawn art form is the whirligig. This folk art form along with the windmill was brought here originally by Northern European settlers. Whirligigs began as primitive whittled dolls with spinning arms, and evolved into intricate mechanisms and a well-documented, early American folk art form (Gladstone, 1974). Today, most whirligigs are made of plastic and purchased at the local discount store or garden center.

The home crafting of lawn art continued as a hobby throughout the years. A 1934 edition of Home Craft magazine offers instructions and patterns for wooden lawn art ranging from storks to hunting dogs. Even today, newspapers and magazines sell woodworking patterns that can be used as "summer garden helpers" and "lawn deco art" (advertisement in The Wichita Eagle, Parade, November 13, 1994).

Lawn art, then as now, served varied purposes. Pieces could be utilitarian as in sundials and planters. Whirligigs or other carved and painted pieces could be the outcome of a craft or hobby. And always, lawn art functioned as a form of expression by embellishing a garden, enlivening a yard or showcasing personal tastes or sentiments.

Through the years trends have changed. The 80's was the decade of the pink flamingo. The

1934 MAGAZINE FOR
DO-IT-YOURSELF LAWN ARTISTS.

A RECENT EXAMPLE OF A WHIRLIGIG CRAFTED FROM WOOD.

once popular lawn jockey, traditionally black-faced, has succumbed to political correctness through either removal or a change of race. But despite trends, a wide variety of lawn art persists, including the standards such as statues of toga-clad Greek women. While lawn art began in formal gardens of the gentry and moved into the everyday realm of folk art, it continues today among all classes. There are no boundaries. Lawn art thrives in urban centers and in rural communities.

Lawn art is also more universal than regional. Regional influences may be noticed but are neither restrictive nor exclusive. Drift wood and sea shells are incorporated in lawn art displays on the coast, but are also used in Kansas. Windmills are likely seen in Kansas, but also show up in lawns in Washington. And Florida's lovely flamingos have definitely migrated to colder climes.

Sometimes a cultural influence will set lawn art apart from the region in which it is displayed. The Dalla horses of Lindsborg, Kansas reflect a Swedish heritage and can be found on homes throughout the country. Pagodas from the far East and clay pottery from Mexico signify cultural pride that stands apart from regional settings.

Whether fine art, folk art, a money-making hobby or an arrangement of whirligigs picked up on sale at discount stores, lawn art is an enduring art form that will likely remain as long as there are yards to decorate.

THE GIRL WITH URN IS A
MODIFIED REPRESENTATION OF
EARLY HELLENISTIC INFLUENCES.

THESE COLUMNS SAVED FROM DEMOLITION NOW GRACE THE GARDEN AS COLUMNS HAVE PLAYED AN IMPORTANT ARCHITECTURAL ROLE THROUGHOUT HISTORY. THIS IS IN CONTRAST TO THE MORE MODERN PAINTED, WOODEN TULIPS.

FLAMINGOES COME IN MANY FORMS USING A VARIETY OF MATERIALS, FROM 1-DIMENSIONAL WOOD CUTOUTS TO ORNATE PAPER MACHE, FROM PLASTIC TO METAL. THIS IS THE MOST COMMON FLAMINGO.

TWO VERSIONS OF THE ONCE POPULAR "REFLECTIVE BALL ON PEDESTAL" THAT IS RETURNING TO POPULARITY.

THESE VERSIONS INCLUDE BOWLING BALLS RATHER THAN A MORE FRAGILE REFLECTIVE BALL THAT DOES NOT STAND UP WELL IN KANSAS HAIL STORMS.

A BLACK-SKINNED LAWN JOCKEY.

A LIGHT-SKINNED LAWN JOCKEY.

LAWN ART AS A REGIONAL MELTING POT: SEA SHELLS FROM THE COAST,
ANTLERS FROM THE MOUNTAINS, SUNFLOWER FROM THE PLAINS.

PAGODA REFLECTS JAPANESE INFLUENCE.

9

TRADITIONAL DONKEY WITH WOODEN CART.

Donkey and Cart
CHAPTER 2

If there were a Top 40 list of popular lawn art, the cart-pulling donkey, known as Pedro, would certainly win an award for longevity. This style of lawn art saw its beginning in the 1940's and was at its height of popularity in the 50's and early 60's. It still remains a popular piece.

The Donkey and Cart was such an appealing piece when it first hit the market that theft became an issue to the owners. The Hanzliceks, for instance, had to chain their second donkey to the front yard light pole. The first donkey purchased in 1959 was stolen. Soon after it disappeared, Mrs. Hanzlicek spotted the stolen donkey in someone else's front yard. She recalls asking her husband to let her out of the car in order to confront the thieves. After all, it was her donkey! Fortunately Mr. Hanzlicek was less emotional about the stolen ornament and refused to stop the car. Upon reflection, Mrs. Hanzlicek now sees the wisdom in her husband's decision, and the humor in the entire incident.

Mr. Hanzlicek still wonders how anyone stole it in the first place. Those donkeys are incredibly heavy—made from cement.

The original "Donkey and Cart" is still made at a nearby cement and concrete retailer. The mold has a copyright and must be purchased from The Concrete Machinery Co., Inc. in Hickory, North Carolina. The company has been in business since the 1940's manufacturing around 500 molds including the Donkey and Cart, one of their oldest molds.

Both the original and imitations of the Donkey and Cart remain a standard in lawn art selection. There are painted and unpainted ones. Some carts are filled with flowers, some with nothing. One cart carries a ceramic duck as a passenger. Most donkeys and carts are American made, although many are made in Mexico offering a south-of-the-border wrought iron styling. The display may include donkey, cart and sometimes a little boy driving the cart or merely sitting to one side.

A common problem for Donkey and Cart owners is breakage. The ears are generally the first to go. Sometimes the damage is extensive and only one piece of the original set remains displayed. On one occasion, neighbors combined their unbroken pieces to make a new complete set.

The Hanzliceks' donkey was an original, painted white to match their house. They had their second donkey for years. With stolid patience, that donkey gave countless rides to the Hanzlicek children and the rest of the kids on the block. Finally, after losing his ears, probably due to one of the kids, he was put to rest, having served long and well.

CLAY DONKEY WITH WROUGHT IRON CART FROM MEXICO.

A STUBBORN MULE.

HITCHING A RIDE.

MINIATURE WINDMILL.

Preserving the Past
CHAPTER 3

An important by-product of lawn art—sometimes intentional, sometimes not—is preserving the past. And the past, for most Americans, implies a rural connection. On her inner-city, postage-stamp sized yard, Marlene keeps a miniature replica of a windmill. When asked why, she replies, "Oh, it's cute." Then, as though the thought just dawned on her, "It reminds me of Grandma's farm. It used to be that was her only source of water."

Many people who display rustic pieces of lawn art never lived on a farm, but their grandparents or parents did. For others the ties are more in spirit than actual. Even though grandma and grandpa lived in town, in a cultural sense we all share a rural ancestry.

For those whose rural connections are real, the tales that accompany their lawn art are educational, if not interesting. When inquiring about an antique plow displayed on a front lawn, the owner began by explaining that his grandfather used a plow just like that one when he first settled in Kansas. And, as usual, the memories poured.

"Well, my grandfather's plow was just a little larger. He always kept it real clean 'cause he was so proud to be the first in the area to have this brand of plow. It was sort of a ritual to sharpen the plow blade. My uncle would come over to help and that meant the cousins would come along, too. Boy, did we ever have some fun. We swam in the creek, fished...."

BARBED WIRE BALL.

When asked about his unique planters, another gentleman replied that they were cream separators. His wife volunteered that "they were just like the ones we used on the farm when I was a girl, only ours were much bigger." Her husband continued, "They're getting really hard to find these days. No one uses them any more." The cream separators in their yard were purchased at the estate sales of farmers who had passed away.

CREAM SEPARATOR PLANTER WITH INSULATORS
IN BACKGROUND.

As the couple reflected on the changing times, the husband mused, "Young people today don't appreciate things like this." "You know, when we die," he said with a grin, "this stuff will be one of the first things the kids get rid of."

Not only are the tales of farm life, but also of simpler times. Glass telephone insulators are displayed in many yards. A simple comment about the insulators' unique shades of green and blue inspire many stories about the old telephone systems, party lines, and the operator who knew everyone and everything about the community. Some people will go so far as to describe their telephone "ring." One residence might answer to "long-short-long," while another's ring would be "short-short-long." People recalled the old phone system as a good way to inform the whole community at once. The operator simply rang the "community number" which summoned all parties to the line.

For many, the lawn is a good place to display antiques and primitives that are too large to fit into a house—wagons and sleighs, for example. For others it is an extension of the "country" mode of interior decorating. A plow is set in a garden with a roll of barbed wire casually slung over the guide handle. Ten and twenty-five gallon crocks are used as planters. So are coal buckets, wash tubs and old cisterns. Often these items are left in their original form; other times they are tole painted or otherwise decorated.

A relatively new form of lawn art involves the use of parts of farm implements to create new sculptures. Tines from rakes are welded together and painted hot pink to create larger-than-life flamingos. Tractor seats, shovels, and even parts of tricycles are used to construct whimsical katydids, magpies and creatures that may have come from Mars.

CREAM SEPARATOR STANDS ALONE.

ANTIQUE PLOW BEHIND GRINDSTONE.

A DIFFERENT TYPE OF INSULATOR USED AS A BIRD FEEDER/BATH.

OLD-FASHIONED ROAD GRADER.

COAL BUCKET PLANTER.

Washtub as a planter with American flag in kettle below.

MAGPIE MADE FROM SHOVEL.

FLAMINGO CREATED FROM OLD RAKE TINES.

25

AIRPLANE PART AS PLANTER.

Acquisition
CHAPTER 4

When finding outstanding works of lawn art, two questions begged to be answered. "Where did all this come from?" And "Why?" It is in the answers to these questions that the most entertaining stories unfold.

"I was driving down the alley and nearly ran over it," volunteered one lawn artist. "Turns out it was part of an airplane. So I took it home and made a planter out of it. Don't know how that thing ever got in the alley in the first place." And sure enough, a shiny, cone-shaped planter brimming with marigolds triumphantly hangs in the middle of the yard.

The "find" is not always as dramatic as driving over something in the alley, but it is often as haphazard. Many lawn art collections are created from the leftovers of a "lot," a box of articles purchased at an auction or estate sale. After sorting out the intended purchases, some people have difficulty parting with the remaining items. So while a chipped teapot would not be displayed in a china cabinet, it makes a lovely planter for the yard. The top of an artificial Christmas tree, surrounded by barnyard fowl and plastic flowers is one artist's use for such odds and ends.

One such collection of garage sale castoffs was placed at the base of a tree that was "hard to mow around anyway," according to a young couple. The husband built a frame to create edging for the lawn and a display area for the newly acquired lawn art pieces. With the display area defined, they now add other pieces that make up a perfect collection. So, in a sense, the lawn art is not static, but an evolving form of expression.

The saying, "one man's trash is another man's treasure," can certainly be applied to the field of lawn art. Recycling is a major motivator for many lawn artists. Recycled two-liter pop bottles and bleach bottles are a common sight. By slitting the sides, bending out "wings," the bottles can be hung from a fishing swivel to become twirling works of art. Recycled art can be as simple as tieing orange plastic newspaper wrappers to wagon wheels, a technique one woman uses to brighten her yard. A more prevalent form of recycled art involves making planters out of old tires, water heaters and washing machine tubs.

Recycled art can be purchased at craft sales and church bazaars. Proud grandparents will happily display recycled art made by their grandchildren. When questioned about an unidentifiable red object hanging from her porch, one mother replied, "I don't know what it is, but my son made it fifteen years ago. I don't dare take it down."

For many other people, the lawn art selections are not as spontaneous. Pieces are painstakingly chosen as supplementary components of landscaping. Generally these pieces, purchased at garden centers or statuary stores, meld into the landscape and serve as accent pieces. The placement is intentional and often quite subtle such as a bird bath or fountain tucked away in a flower garden, a small gnome figurine peering out from under a bush, or a set of fawns resting under a shady tree.

A trip to Mexico is the story behind numerous pieces of lawn art. It might be a souvenir from a once-in-a-lifetime vacation, or additions regularly updated on trips to visit family. Lawn art is relatively inexpensive and abundant in Mexican border towns. Donkeys, planters and statuary can be found in either unpainted clay or brightly painted ceramic. Wrought iron is also a popular buy.

It's not necessary to travel to a foreign country, however, to purchase lawn art. As already noted, pieces can be purchased at garage sales, craft shows, and garden centers. Lawn art for sale can also be found as near as a neighbor's front yard. Many lawn artists create and paint wooden yard ornaments and place them in their yards to entice potential customers. One of the most common wooden ornaments is the "bent-over gardener." She comes in a variety of heights and dress, although her attire usually includes a red and white polka-dotted dress with white undies. Wooden tulips, life-size cows, and wooden children swinging from painted swings are easy to spot and often for sale.

PLANTER MADE FROM OLD TIRE.

Whether purchased or hand-made, many collections of lawn art are chosen as part of a theme. Country is a popular interior and exterior decorating theme. Farmyard fowl in cement or ceramic, a large old rendering kettle filled with petunias, or cream cans painted in coordinating colors can lend a country feel to a home. Another popular subject is a woodland theme including deer and maybe a forest elf or two. Sometimes yard art reminds the owner of the past, or declares a cultural heritage. Windmills connect us to the prairie, as driftwood and sea shells reflect life on the coast. Other times yard art reminds the owners of a place they would rather be. Rugged, carved bears and mountain creatures line the walk to a house, pronouncing the city dwellers' love of the Rockies, although hundreds of miles away.

Lawn art may make other statements, too. Religious art proclaims the beliefs of many home owners. Most examples of religious art are statues of Jesus, Mary or a favorite saint displayed in a garden, on a bird bath or in a grotto. The grottos can be quite sophisticated with glass front enclosures, decorated with flowers and stones, or as simple as a bathtub, cut in half and propped on end enshrining a Madonna. Some people create patriotic landscapes and turn their yards into political billboards, displaying posters or Uncle Sam in red-white-and-blue.

Other lawn art themes are equally as specific, but merely for fun. Frogs are a favorite. Lawn artists may limit exhibits to only one type of art. A collection of turtles is displayed in a neighbor's yard. A dark glass turtle rests on a rock. A small green turtle hides under a plant. These turtles were collected over the years, often received as gifts.

Lawn art collections can become ongoing hobbies. Additions to a collection are picked up as souvenirs while traveling, discovered at craft sales and gardening centers, or fashioned from finds at estate sales and auctions. People who collect lawn art find that they soon begin receiving lawn articles as Christmas or birthday gifts from friends and family.

From the perspective of a gift-giver, shopping for a lawn art collector is a relatively easy task. From the perspective of the gift-receiver, this may become a problem. Even though a gift may be intended for the yard, it may not suit the lawn artist's tastes. What does one do with a well-intentioned gift such as a plastic, grey hippopotamus planter? Another problem may be satura-

CREATIVE USE OF LEFTOVERS.

tion. Just how many geese statues can one lawn accommodate?

There are lawn artists, however, who view any addition to their lawn art collections as a welcome treasure. There is no saturation point; there is room in their yards and in their hearts for absolutely anything that comes their way.

WHIRLIGIG TREE MADE FROM RECYCLED POPBOTTLES.

A COLLECTION OF BUNNIES.

CREATIVE USE OF OLD TENNIS BALLS AND INSTITUTIONAL FLOOR BUFFERS.

RENDERING KETTLE WITH WAGON WHEEL PLANTER.

LU'S FAVORITE: THE HOT WATER HEATER CONVERTED INTO PLANTER.

PROUDLY DISPLAYED, UNIDENTIFIABLE ART PROJECT MADE BY SON.

Garden gnome.

DEER STATUARY FOUND IN MANY LAWNS.

STATUARY BROUGHT BACK BY FAMILY FROM A RELATIVE'S STORE IN MEXICO.

COMMON AND UNCOMMON BENT-OVER GARDENERS.

41

CRAFT PROJECTS AS LAWN ART MADE FOR FUN OR PROFIT.

DOMESTICATED URBAN COW.

CREAM CAN TRIO AS BIRDBATH.

PLASTER ROOSTER.

AX CARVED WOODEN ROOSTER.

A VARIETY OF WINDMILLS.

WOOD CARVINGS OF MOUNTAIN CREATURES.

MADONNA.

GARDEN GUARDIAN.

COVERING ALL THE BASES.

St. Francis and a squirrel.

MARY UNDER GLASS.

POLITICS AND PATRIOTISM.

STAR-SPANGLED BUTTERFLY.

RED, WHITE AND BLUE FENCE PROCLAIMS POLITICAL PREFERENCES.

LADY LIBERTY BLOCKS THE GARAGE.

VARIATIONS OF EVER-POPULAR FROG LAWN ORNAMENTS.

JUST ONE OF A TURTLE COLLECTION.

VIEW OF YODER'S ORNAMENTAL CONCRETE, A STATUARY SHOP AND FACTORY LOCATED IN BURRTON, KANSAS.

RECYCLED PART BECOMES PLANTER.

LAWN ART ARRANGEMENTS THAT CONTINUE TO DEVELOP.

LINCOLNVILLE, KANSAS

Tending Lawn Art
CHAPTER 5

People are involved in their lawn art to various degrees. Some people display a piece or two periodically, perhaps a wooden reindeer or Nativity scene at Christmas. For others one piece of permanently displayed art may suffice, a birdbath or a statue of St. Francis. But what brings true delight to the lawn art fan is the bold soul whose creative fancies pour forth across the lawn and into the bushes. These are the true lawn artists.

Over one hundred pieces, lined up in eight rows fill the front yard of a farm near Lincolnville, Kansas. Grouped according to themes, one sees bears, cartoon figures, flamingoes, assorted fowl, deer, pigs, frogs and other identifiable and abstract works of art. The collection is so extensive and so orderly that many people mistake it for a sales display. Hence the sign, "Lawn Art Not For Sale," wards off would-be customers at the entrance to the driveway.

Driving past a masterpiece collection of lawn art is like watching a three-ring circus. While the vibrancy and excitement grab the eye, concentration and focus are needed to enjoy the individual acts. Technique and creativity are noticed only when you stop to explore each piece in the collection.

Mrs. Shepherd wraps bits of aluminum foil around objects to better catch the sunlight. Wads of foil are stuffed inside green plastic 2-liter bottles for another glittering effect. She balances

SEA ZEBRA BIRD BATH.

smooth round rocks in the mouths of plastic frogs and then places them atop pedestals for an amusing effect. The rocks also keep her works in place despite strong, Midwestern winds. Plastic daffodils sprout out of old, lead pipes. A grouping of Planters Peanuts dolls, an arrangement of sea shells and antlers, and a black-faced clown in an antique wagon wheel delight both the viewer and the artist. In the center ring, a life-size horse, wearing a multi-colored crocheted blanket, looks past a ceramic clown head resting on a pink plastic lawn chair.

USES OF ALUMINUM FOIL.

The upkeep of these collections, while an enjoyable hobby, is also tedious. Like a garden, each work of art is planted in just the right spot. The collection is tended with great care and concern. No matter how unwieldy the collection, the grass is neatly trimmed around each piece.

Each season brings on different chores for the lawn artist. Summer means edging, edging and more edging. It also means setting up pieces blown over in a summer storm and securing pieces that fall victim to vandals' hands during idle summer nights.

During the winter, bird baths and fountains are drained. Vulnerable art is covered with plastic or stored in the garage. Holiday pieces are added for festive occasions. Front-porch lions and geese don hats and mufflers.

And finally, spring sees a fresh coat of paint on the pump handle under the windmill. Leaves from last fall are dug out of Pedro's donkey cart. Flowers are planted. And like a garden, the well-tended collection grows throughout the year. Old pieces are weeded out and new pieces are added—a gift received at Christmas, a tractor seat found at a farm auction, a sculpture discovered at the local farm and art market, an empty bottle of bubble bath.

A YARD FULL OF ART

BUCKET ENHANCED WITH WIREFRAME AND PLASTIC BALLS
TOPPED WITH ALUMINUM FOIL

ROCKS IN AND ON THINGS.

ELEPHANT, SHELLS, WIRE, ANTLERS, INSULATORS AND MUCH MORE.

WOODEN TULIPS BLOOM YEAR ROUND.

PLASTIC DAFFODILS SPROUT FROM LEAD PIPES.

A FLOCK OF FLAMINGOS GRAZE OVER A WELL-MANICURED LAWN.

Seashell mosaic.

LITTLE BOY WHO BELONGS IN BIRD BATH IS KEPT
INSIDE TO PREVENT THEFT.

LAWN ART PROTECTED FROM THIEVES.

CHRISTMAS ART—THE SIMPLE, THE RIDICULOUS AND THE SUBLIME.

More Halloween creations.

Santa's sleigh led by flamingos.

THE RELIGIOUS BLENDS WITH THE SECULAR.

A FRESH COAT OF PAINT HERALDS SPRING'S ARRIVAL.

FALL LEAF RAKING CAN BE A CHALLENGE FOR LAWN ARTISTS.

MOTOR FAN FLOWER.

Fish swimming across backyard fence.

CHRISTMAS LIGHTS—THE MOST COMMON FORM OF LAWN ART.

LIVE CAT POSES WITH LAWN ART.

A COWBOY NEAR LINCOLNVILLE.

Conclusion
CHAPTER 6

Lawn artists are divided into four basic categories. The first, and largest, category includes those who select lawn ornamentation for their garden much as a homeowner purchases an oil painting or print to hang behind the living room sofa.

The second category includes artists who either dabble or seriously study fine arts and display their sculptures outside. Some sculptors limit their displays to their own yards. For others, their pieces may be displayed in a variety of places, with only one or two sculptures finding a home at home. Sometimes the sculpture displayed is a "just for fun" piece. Perhaps it's not up to the usual artistic standards of excellence, but something the artist liked anyhow and kept for the garden. Other times, a piece is displayed to intice potential buyers.

A third category of lawn artists includes those who have never studied the fine arts, but become artist's through their work in the yard. Some find inspiration through their occupations. One farmer creates a giant turkey out of a hay bale. Along Highway 56, a farmer has put together a gigantic grasshopper using parts of large farm machinery. He has also designed several deer and buffalo. Other lawn artists find creative outlets for their welding expertise, creating a variety of sculptures from scrap metals and junk yard parts.

A notable example of this type of artist can by found in Lucas, Kansas at the "Garden of

Eden" created by S.P. Dinsmoor. An outstanding display of lawn art was created over years by this Civil War veteran and school teacher. He listed his occupation as a farmer.

Beginning in 1907 Dinsmoor formed cement sculptures to express his views of the Creation Story, U.S. politics and economics, and life in general. His works cover the entire property, forming fences, arbors, animal cages, flower beds and even a mausoleum. Amazingly Dinsmoor did not begin his work until he was 64 years old. By 1927, he had used over 113 tons of cement in developing his masterpiece. His house and garden are preserved as an historical site, with tours given regularly. Although, one can pass by at any time and observe this major work of lawn art.

And lastly, there are lawn artists who neither weld nor sculpt nor build. These are the people who create great collages in their lawns. They put together intricate displays using an endless array of materials. These are the yards we remember, the yards that cause passing cars to slow down in amazement. These are the places that come to mind when someone mentions the words "lawn art."

SCULPTURE PLANTED IN A GARDEN.

A SCULPTED WREATH.

The "Marlboro Man" from Florence, Kansas.

A MAN'S HOME IS NOT ALWAYS HIS CASTLE.

IRON BUFFALO CLIMB ROCK PILE.

EARL SLAGLE CREATED MOTORIZED SCULPTURES AFTER MEASURING A COW SKELETON FROM THE VETERINARY DEPARTMENT AT KANSAS STATE UNIVERSITY.

COWS MOVE HEADS AS THOUGH THEY WERE GRAZING.

REGAL LION GUARDS AFFLUENT NEIGHBORHOOD.

A DOG PILE.

DEER LEAP FENCE INTO HENRY'S SCULPTURE HILL.

Eagle weather vane.

CISTERN AND CREAM CAN.

CLAY FISH.

Prairie jesters and an antique plow with old barbed wire.

A buffalo roams near Highway 56.

Antique manure spreader.

A CREATION BY A FARMER NEAR BURRTON, KANSAS. THE HORSE HAS BEEN SCULPTED USING WINDOW SCREENS AND OTHER MATERIALS.

TURKEY IN THE STRAW.

CLAY CREATIONS FROM MEXICO.

EXAMPLES OF A UNIQUE LAWN ART COLLECTION.

A UNIQUE PIECE.

LINCOLNVILLE IS FOR LOOKERS ONLY.

TIRE PLANTER.

POTTERY PURCHASED IN MEXICO.

HALLOWEEN DECORATION MADE BY 18-YEAR OLD. MOTHER REPORTED THAT SON RECEIVED A NUMBER OF CALLS.

A CIRCUS OF ART.

PRANCING METAL PONY.

BLACK-FACED CLOWN IN ANTIQUE WAGON WHEEL.

INSULATORS ON ANTIQUE YOKE COMBINED WITH MANY MODERN ELEMENTS.

INSULATORS IN BEDSPRINGS.

Concrete angel atop mausoleum where Dinsmoor and wife are laid to rest. Garden of Eden, Lucas, Kansas.

Bibliography

Dinsmoor, S.P. Pictorial History of The Cabin Home in Garden of Eden. Kansas, Lucas.

Gladstone, M.J. (1974). A Carrot for a Nose: The Form of Folk Sculpture on America's City Streets and Country Roads. New York: Charles Scribner's Sons.

Holman, Rhonda (1995, August 6). Art Around Us: Henry's Sculpture Hill. The Wichita Eagle, p. D1.

Plumptre, George (1989). Garden Ornament: Five Hundred Years of Nature, Art, and Artifice. New York: Doubleday.

Thomas, Judy Lundstrom (1994, October 31). No Bones About It: He's a Little Different. The Wichita Eagle, p. C1.